ONE HUNDRED AND FIFTEEN COPIES
OF THIS PRIVATE EDITION HAVE BEEN
PRINTED ON ALEXANDRIA VELLUM
FROM COMPOSITION DONE BY THE
PHILOPOLIS PRESS, SAN FRANCISCO,
THE TYPE AFTERWARDS DISTRIBUTED

This copy is Number

Retracing the Pioneers

MISSION DOLORES, SAN FRANCISCO

"OUR STARTING POINT"

Retracing the Pioneers

FROM WEST TO EAST
IN AN AUTOMOBILE

BY

HUGO ALOIS TAUSSIG

PRIVATELY PRINTED
SAN FRANCISCO, 1910

To My Friends

IF I have failed to devote space in the following pages to descriptions of the country we travelled through nd the people we met, it must not be inferred that we vere unobserving. The truth is, that crossing the American Continent affords one but little variety of incident. As or the people we met, I can truthfully say that we met no Indians on our way across the Continent, and that the ountry harbored no such people as our interesting California '49er, the ubiquity of the railroad having made the ntire people as one, and the numberless hotels mitigating gainst meeting with the old time hospitality of the farmer. The Trans-Continental trip was made under our own ower, with ROBERT R. SHERMAN at the wheel, and vith occasional assistance from my travelling companions HENRY E. DIGGLES and THOMAS J. KELLY.

HUGO A. TAUSSIG

SAN FRANCISCO, *January 2, 1910*

The Illustrations

The Illustrations

Retracing the Pioneers

WITH a turn of the crank we were off on a tour across the American Continent in an automobile. No! not for the purpose of making a record — just for pleasure. Did we get it? I leave it to my readers to judge. We left San Francisco on the first day of June. A beautiful gray day cheered us on our way. We did not get further than two or three hundred yards from our starting point when we recorded our first experience. In the excitement of taking leave we allowed our engine to die and forgot to release the clutch in making the street crossing, and in order to avoid being run down by a street car resorted to man power, with the result that we started our engine with no one at the wheel. St. Christopher, our patron Saint, and the presence of mind of one of our party saved us from a disastrous exit from San Francisco.

Our natural gateway — the State road between Placerville and the Nevada Line being

1

closed to us owing to snow on the summit, we wended our way south, making our starting point in San Francisco at the Mission Dolores, thence via El Camino Real or Mission Road, with its many truck farms, past the country homes of San Mateo into the fertile Santa Clara Valley, with its many orchards and seed farms, on to the Mission San Juan Bautista. After a hurried visit to this interesting Mission we made the run over the San Juan grade, which afforded us some very pretty views of the San Benito Valley, into the Salinas Valley, where at Soledad we took the old stage route through the picturesque Jolon and Indian Valleys, reaching Mission San Miguel at twilight. With a good road before us and an inviting hotel as our incentive, we ran on to Paso Robles for the night, recording 221.5 miles for this our first day's run.

MISSION SAN GABRIEL

Retracing the Pioneers

EARLY morning of the second day saw us continuing along the old stage route to Santa Margarita and over a steep and winding mountain pass to Mission San Luis Obispo. With a choice of routes from San Luis Obispo, we took the more interesting route along the Pacific Ocean to Pismo Beach. Here we again left the coast for the vegetable producing section of San Luis Obispo County, and the bean, sugar beet and oil producing section of Santa Barbara County to Los Olivos. The choice of roads again being ours, and mindful of the fact that ere long our path across the Continent would take us away from the coast, we sacrificed good roads and mountain scenery for marine views. Not until after we had enjoyed the Santa Ynez Mission and its olive groves, the beautiful wooded country, the mountain streams and the Gaviota Pass did we appreciate how much we had sacrificed for marine views. Running along the coast we were obliged to " negotiate " numerous arroyos, which some witty soul had named " the fifty-

5

seven varieties". They certainly were most trying varieties, though they did afford us the pleasure of helping some poor unfortunate motorist whom lack of power had stalled along the road. I may mention that had it not been for such experiences the trip across the Continent would have been most monotonous. Thanks to Santa Barbara County we spent an eventful and pleasant afternoon running over its poor roads from Gaviota to Goleta. We arrived at Santa Barbara with our odometer at 147.8 miles.

MISSION SANTA BARBARA

Retracing the Pioneers

LEAVING Santa Barbara and its picturesque Mission behind us, we set out
for the metropolis of Southern California. Following along State Street and the
Ocean Boulevard, our road led us through
Montecito Valley with its many pretty homes
and parks on to Summerland with its oil wells
extending out into the ocean. Five miles
further on saw us amidst orange groves, and
but few miles more and we were climbing
over the Casitas Pass into Ventura County.
With good roads before us we were not long
running over the Conejo and Cahuenga
Passes to Los Angeles, a distance from Santa
Barbara of 104.9 miles.

Retracing the Pioneers

HAVING equipped ourselves with burlap, block and tackle, pick and shovel, and a goodly supply of edibles, we left Los Angeles on the morning of the fifth day. Following the line of the Southern Pacific to Fernando we passed over the very steepest grade of the entire trip, Newhall Pass, through Soledad Canyon on to Palmdale. Here we left the line of the railroad for Del Sur. I do not know that I have any real reason for mentioning Del Sur other than that it marked the place where a kindly store-keeper allowed us the use of empty sugar barrels and boxes to spread our lunch upon, from our own larder. After voting this, our first outdoor luncheon, a success, we ran on to Willow Springs and Mojave, a distance from Los Angeles of 114.6 miles.

THE ROAD NEAR SANTA BARBARA

Retracing the Pioneers

KNOWING the nature of the desert country before us, we made an early morning start from Mojave and followed the line of the Los Angeles aqueduct, now in course of construction. We, however, had not proceeded further than Red Rock Canyon, a short distance out of Mojave, when we ran into a stretch of about one hundred and fifty yards of sand, which stalled our motor. This being our first experience, we were somewhat at a loss just how to proceed, but after some thought threw the combined strength of three men against the rear end of our car, and literally pushed the car out of the sand and on a more solid bottom, and continued on our way. Our joy was not of long duration, for at Grape Vine, not more than thirty miles further, we came to what we supposed a fork in the roads, and there being no apparent choice, we took the right fork and ran into trouble more serious than our first experience of the day. Pushing and pulling would not budge our car, as it did in the first instance, so not until we wore our-

13

selves out did the thought come to us that we had fortified ourselves against just such an occurrence by equipping ourselves with burlap. We cut the burlap into long strips about eighteen inches wide, the ends of which we tucked under the wheels of the machine. After weighting down the burlap at different intervals, we announced to our driver that we were ready for him; that at a certain signal he should "turn her loose". The signal given, away went the car, but we saw our burlap being torn to the extent of worthlessness for any further use. Burlap is not bad if you can pack it in sufficient quantities to say good-bye to it as you spread it on the road. I would, however, suggest a heavy canvas cut in long strips two feet in width as a more economical and serviceable equipment for desert motoring. Although in the desert, we found great interest in watching the stupendous work of Los Angeles capital in building the aqueduct. From Grape Vine we ran on to Little Lake and Haiwee, a fertile spot in the desert, and a most inviting place for spreading our lunch and enjoying a

NEWHALL PASS

good cigar and a siesta. Profiting by our forenoon's experience, we were more successful in covering a stretch of seven miles, more or less, beyond Haiwee, of bad sand. This, however, was accomplished at the cost of a cut tire and pinched tube. After a delay of forty minutes we ran on to Olancha, near Owens Lake, and then into the fertile valley of the Owens River. Snow covered Mount Whitney to our left, and cultivation and the river to our right were welcome and beautiful sights after many miles of desert. Fourteen miles more, and with 132.5 miles as our day's run, we ran into Independence for the night.

SAND STRETCH, GRAPE VINE

Retracing the Pioneers

EXPECTING that we would profit by the advice of knowing ones, we took the lane or upper road out of Independence and blindly followed directions through mud and water into depths we feared. Thinking discretion the better part of valor, we concluded to reverse our engine. A lucky thought took us to a road paralleling the C. & C. R. R., which ere long brought us into Big Pine. Here we took on gasoline, filled our water bags and thermos bottles, and after making enquiries as to the roads, took the grade over the White Mountains, which afforded us a pretty view of the valley of the Owens River, and which soon led us away from habitation and railroads and into Mono County. After travelling for some time we reached Foreman's Ranch, Oasis. Cookhouse odors and our appetites, suggested the noon hour. I need not add that we were not long hunting the cookhouse and what it afforded us. "Four bits per" bought us a seat at the "Table d'hote" dinner, served on a long table devoid of tablecloth and napkins.

OASIS, MONO COUNTY, NEAR CALIFORNIA-NEVADA LINE

Having satisfied our appetites, we studied human nature by " gluing our eyes " on one individual who, we finally concluded, was a brother of Buffalo Bill, if " get up " counted for anything. Dinner over, we hunted up the foreman of the ranch for further road directions, and off we were. At 2:30 that afternoon we reached the California-Nevada State Line, having travelled a distance from San Francisco of about 788.8 miles, or about 500 miles further than we would have been

19

obliged to travel had we taken the Placerville-Tahoe road. After crossing the State Line our first town in the Sage Brush State was the partially deserted mining town Silver Peak. According to our directions we were following the tracks of an automobile which had left Oasis ahead of us, and which we were told was bound for Tonopah, our destination for that night. Although it seemed to us that we were bearing too much to the south we followed the tracks, and much to our surprise, ran into Goldfield, one of Nevada's liveliest mining towns. The day was quite a strenuous one, as we had surmounted five summits, and the Goldfield Hotel looked inviting to us, and with 128.2 miles for the day's run, we put up for the night.

Retracing the Pioneers

PLEASED with our unexpected visit to Goldfield, and enjoying the comforts of a good hotel, we pulled out the next morning at ten-thirty for the run to Tonopah, another lively and interesting mining town, but 25.6 miles away.

The real "dyed-in-the-wool" Western hospitality, and a bunch of jolly good fellows kept us in Tonopah for the day.

Retracing the Pioneers

KNOWING that a mining engineer, well acquainted with the roads and cut-offs, intended starting out in his Simplex machine over a portion of the road we were to cover, we got under way at five in the morning, and at Stone Cabin we caught up with his machine. Nine and a half miles further on we recorded our first "tyre blow out", which meant not only the loss of an hour, but also the loss of our guiding machine, which went on ahead. At Stone Cabin our guide, the engineer, told us that at the fork of the roads near an uninhabited spot named Warm Springs, we were no longer to follow his tracks, but were to take the road to the right. On reaching the fork of the roads we saw before us, conspicuously placed on the end of a stick, a piece of paper with the note, "Here is where I leave you, keep right-hand road to Twin Springs".

Arriving at Twin Springs, consisting of a cabin and a small spring, we again halted, this time to change a rear tyre — then fifty-two miles through a tiresome country, with

TWIN SPRINGS

the uncertainty of roads — if trails may be styled roads, as our sole diversion to Blue Eagle. Out of Blue Eagle we ran into a more interesting country, to us full of incidents. We had not travelled further than Curry Creek, thirteen miles away, when we arrived at what appeared to us to be the end of the road. As self-appointed captain of the party, I left the machine for a distant house in search of road information. I got what I was after. Our machine had not made more than one hundred feet when I heard a crash, and looking out I saw the rear wheel of the machine go through a weak culvert. There being no damage to it, we took what fun we could in the labor of getting the machine out of its perilous position.. A few miles further on, while going up a grade, our machine stuck

23

"SUGGESTED A BOTTOMLESS MARSH"

in the sand. However, getting the machine out of sand no longer had any terror for us; for by experience we had gained, that unless the sand was very heavy, by throwing our coil of rope under one or both of the rear or driving wheels, they got traction and with it, locomotion. Out of Barnes, another short run, and we reached what very much suggested a bottomless marsh, the crossing of which did not appear feasible.

Equipped with long pieces of fence rail, we had just commenced sounding the first pool of water when, to our joy, a halfbreed

24

appeared on the scene. He greeted us by "Team got stuck here this morning". We were not long in getting him to take a friendly interest in us and to point out just where the wagon got stalled. Our next move was to find the "High Spots", which we did with the aid of our sticks. With this information, we stationed ourselves on the banks of the pool with ropes and brush in hand ready to assist our machine from getting mired. The landing made, and fearful of a repetition, we engaged the services of the knowing half-breed to pilot us through this stretch of country — about two miles, more or less, being under water. By opening a series of gates, and running across country, we again reached the main highway and dry roads. Twenty-eight miles of good roads took us into Ely, and one mile further to the Steptoe Hotel, East Ely, our odometer registering 182.6 miles for the day's run.

Retracing the Pioneers

TIPPETT, NEVADA

EFORE leaving Ely we were kept busy the entire forenoon making a fruitless search for a tire to replace the extra tire which we were obliged to put on the day before, and which was most essential if we concluded to take the road of the Old Pony Express, and away from the railroad. Relying on our good luck, we at 2:30 that afternoon left Ely to follow the road of the Old Overland Mail, with the information that the stumps of the old telegraph poles would act as our guide. We had not travelled sixty

26

niles when an explosion announced a "tyre
blow out", which was augmented shortly
after by the tyre shoe coming off. We started
out fully expecting to make Ibapah, Utah, by
night, but with the hands of our watch point-
ng at eight, we concluded to put up at
Tippett, recording but 67.7 miles for the
afternoon's run.

DEEP CREEK NEAR IBAPAH, UTAH

A HOUSE, a barn, a few sheep and a
small parcel of cultivated land, is all
that Tippett appeared to be to the
chance passer by. A short visit, however,
soon convinced us that there was more to the
place than we looked for. We found a post
office, a warehouse well stocked with mer-
chandise, and an interesting lot of people.
Puzzled as to what warranted them in ostra-
cizing themselves, as we felt these people had
done, and curiosity getting the better of us,
we made inquiries. Much to our surprise

28

ALKALI FLAT, SKULL VALLEY, OUT OF CALLAO, UTAH

we learned that there were quite a number of farmers and stock men scattered all over the country, who came long distances to transact their business. Nothing of this was visible.

Leaving Tippett, we soon ran into a country which we found under irrigation, and on to roads which were under water. But a few miles further saw us in Ibapah, Utah, which supported a store, demonstrating to us that we were passing through an inhabited country. The next twenty miles did not afford us much of interest, the only life we saw being an occasional antelope, bands of

29

wild horses and coyotes. At noon we ran into Willow Springs, Callao, a Mormon settlement, a very fertile spot on the edge of the Great American Desert. Before leaving we had luncheon in one of the Mormon homes, and a noon day rest. Rest was problematic, owing to the numberless children; but our host assured us that the family a little further along the road could boast of a greater number of children. Eight miles further and our machine was stuck in an alkali flat, and not until we had thrown everything and anything available under the mired wheel, did we succeed in extricating it. Though we had not covered many miles when we reached Thomas Station, Fish Springs, a rather uninviting place, we called it a day's run, with the odometer indicating 70.9 miles.

Retracing the Pioneers

RUINS OF A STATION ON THE OLD OVERLAND ROUTE

THOMAS Station not affording us much other than fighting gnats, poor food and unclean beds, innocent of linen, and knowing that we had a run of fifty miles through the desert before us, we did not tarry long, so at five the next morning we were again under way. We had covered not more than four miles when a tyre blew out, and eighteen miles further on we had a second blow out. With only a much worn out tyre, which we fortunately packed with us in lieu of a new one, we still felt that in an emergency it would see us through our trouble, and to Salt Lake City. At forty-one miles, after having travelled through a country devoid of water, vegetation and habitation, we ran into a lonely stage station where we remained just long enough to brew some coffee for ourselves. At noon we left, and not more than twenty miles later we again heard a familiar sound, which in this instance recorded tyre blow out number three. On went a tyre shoe and another inside protector, and away we went. This time we travelled ten miles, when blow out number four came upon us. After putting our heads together, we finally concluded to cut the bead from the worn out tyre and reinforce the one that was causing us so much trouble, and as an extra precaution we changed our positions in the tonneau so as to remove all weight possible from it. But a run of another hour again saw us in trouble, and we recorded blow out number five. Again we put our tyre in shape, and in fear and trembling moved on. With but eleven miles between our trouble and habitation, we concluded that possibly, with extremely slow running of the machine,

Retracing the Pioneers

THOMAS, FISH SPRINGS, UTAH

and with no load at all, might see us at least
that far. So, barring the driver, the happy
family took to their feet. We made Lookout
Station and in sight of habitation, which
made matters look more cheerful. Our
cheer, however, was not lasting, for a little
further on blow out number six occurred,
and we were on the rim. Luckily we were
out of the desert by this time and in a soft,
moist soil. Since our tyre refused to hold
air, we fed it on rope, tied some to the rim,
and with a smile moved on — only for a short
way, however, then we stuck in the mud.

The efforts of our combined weight shoved our car out, and we were soon hobbling along again. At 6:45 P.M., with 65.6 miles for the day's run, we were in Vernon, a small Mormon settlement but a few miles from the railroad and in easy reach of Salt Lake City, and supplies.

EMERGENCY TYRE REPAIRING IN THE DESERT

Retracing the Pioneers

WITH good bed and board, our enforced rest of a day and a half at Vernon, during our mechanician's trip to Salt Lake City to purchase tubes and tyres, was quite as agreeable as it was unexpected. At noon of the second day we were again equipped, and at three that afternoon under way.

It was not long before we ran into Tooele, where, for the first time in many days, we saw land under cultivation. Little further on, at Garfield, we saw the Great Salt Lake, and with our odometer at 66.2 miles, we ran into Salt Lake City, the first city of any size since leaving Los Angeles, California.

Retracing the Pioneers

IN order to give our mechanician time to overhaul our car, which had not received more than the ordinary care, although it had taken us safely over thirteen hundred miles, and furthermore, being in need of inner tubes and tyres, we delayed a day at Salt Lake City. Properly equipped and our machine overhauled, we pulled out of Salt Lake City on the morning of the sixteenth day at ten o'clock. We had travelled not more than a few miles when we ran into a beautiful fertile valley with snow covered mountains in the distance; and ever mindful of our appetites, made a slight detour to reach Ogden and its restaurants. After luncheon we ran back to Riverdale and on through the scenic Weber canyon, with its winding roads crossing and recrossing its running streams. Needless to say we did not fail to see the Devil's Slide, so well known to the patrons of the Union Pacific. After a most interesting and enjoyable run through Weber Canyon, we passed through the more bleak, though romantic, Echo Canyon. When

THE DEVIL'S SLIDE

within a few miles of the Utah-Wyoming Line, at a station on the railroad named Wahsatch, we passed Weston, the pedestrian, on his walk across the American Continent. Though it was after eight that evening when we reached Evanston, our odometer reading was but 117.7 miles for the day, showing that we took advantage of what the day afforded us, and manifested appreciation of it after nigh eight hundred miles of desert travelling.

EVANSTON, WYOMING

Retracing the Pioneers

WHILE in Salt Lake City we tried to get our route through Wyoming. All the response we received to our many inquiries was: "See P. W. Spaulding, the attorney at Evanston; he has made the trip across the Continent". We lost no time looking him up and he kindly furnished us with a map of the country, on which he traced the route we were to take. He being an automobile enthusiast, and as it was Thursday night, we induced him to take a week's end run with us. We shipped our luggage in order to gain seating space and lighten our load, and at the appointed hour the next morning, under his guidance, left the main line of the Union Pacific for the coal mining town, Cumberland, on the Oregon Short Line. Cumberland is in Wyoming and on a railroad, still it harbored a man to whom it was our pleasure to explain the workings of the first automobile he had ever seen.

From Cumberland we went to Opal, and then to Granger, on the main line of the Union Pacific. This road we were to parallel into Omaha, the elements permitting. From here our road took us over a series of washes (gullies), of which Marston Wash was considered the worst, and which we were told we would not be able to cross without the assistance of a team of horses. Good luck, a sixty horse power engine, or good driving, however, took us over the washes and on to Bryan, where we were compelled to take to the railroad ties for a short distance in order to regain our road. With the exception of the replacing of our driving chain, which came off owing to the strenuous travelling, we had no further trouble to Green River. But a few miles more, and with 131.3 miles for our day's work, we were in Rock Springs, our stopping place for the night.

RUNNING MACHINE OVER BURLAP, THROUGH A SANDY STRETCH
WYOMING ROAD

Retracing the Pioneers

POINT OF ROCKS, WYOMING

WE travelled but a few miles out of Rock Springs when we found ourselves fighting our way through a stretch of about two hundred yards of sand. Coils of ropes, all the dry brush we could find, and fifty-five minutes of hard labor conquered it. This, however, was but a suggestion of what was still to come. A party travelling *en auto* bound for Seattle kindly informed us that we had some "dandy ditches" before us. They failed to tell us that a team hauled them over the bad places. We were not long getting our experience. Ditch number one cost us half an hour's tugging, and ditch number two another half hour. Aside from this variation, we spent the entire day running over what purported to be roads, and for pastime watched the Union Pacific track laborers and the semaphores along the track, until at 123 miles we put into Rawlins.

"NEGOTIATING" A WYOMING WASH

Retracing the Pioneers

STALLED IN ELK MOUNTAINS, WYOMING ROAD

AT Rawlins we learned that the bridges were washed out and that the automobilists in the New York-Seattle race were travelling over the railroad bridges with much difficulty and with injury to their machines. Expecting to profit by their experiences, we appealed to our travelling companion, Mr. Spaulding, to direct us around the trouble. Knowing the country, he tried to inform himself as to the condition of the roads, but, not contrary to the usual, he found it almost impossible to get authentic information. He finally concluded to make a detour of over forty miles, so at eight-thirty the next

OUR HOSTS IN ELK MOUNTAINS, WYOMING

morning we were heading south and away from the main line of the Union Pacific. Our road took us *via* Hopkins Ranch through unfrequented canyons to Saratoga. Delighted with our forenoon's successful run we, after a noon day rest, moved on. We had not proceeded far when we were caught in a thunder storm which came upon us very suddenly. After hurriedly adjusting our storm curtains, we speeded on to Schoojan's Ranch, where we found the country for some distance around under water. With the assurance that there was bottom to the road and with Mr. Schoojan's directions well jotted down, we put on our skid chains and moved on. We were not out of sight of the ranch when we discovered a puncture. Our puncture repaired, we braved three miles of hog-back road which our machinery at times failed to clear in spite of thirteen and a half inches clearance, when much to our dismay, our rear wheels went almost out of sight in the mud and we were stuck. With the rain beating down on us we set to work to extricate our machine. We got our right wheel

47

partly jacked up, when in looking at the left wheel we found that the only obstruction that kept it from going out of sight was the axle. This, however, did not discourage us, and we continued our good work by building up underneath it until it was on a solid foundation. Then we turned our attention to the left wheel, which we also propped up. With our rear wheels high and dry, our next thought was how to pull the machine to firm ground. Our block and tackle we found could not be used, for we could not gain a hold for our "dead-man". The only thing left us being our own strength, we tied a rope to the front axle, and with four men on the rope, the machine in the low, and with a full throttle, we pulled her out. Leaving our machine, we walked on to a sheepherder's wagon in search of road information from its lonely occupants, with the usual success. Failing in this we started off over the road afoot. We had not far to go before we found that the road was impassable for any kind of a vehicle. It being five in the afternoon, we finally concluded to tie up for the night, satisfied that if Elk Mountain afforded us no shelter other than our machine, the sheep-herders at least offered to satisfy the inner man. After our repast, which consisted of mutton stew and coffee, we borrowed our host's shoes to replace our well soaked pedal covers, took our mileage for the day, 57.4 miles, and piled into our automobile for the night.

OUR NIGHT'S ABODE IN ELK MOUNTAINS, WYOMING

Retracing the Pioneers

ETWIXT spinning yarns and occasional naps we managed to pass the night, and were not sorry to see the dawn of day. Unable to continue as originally planned, and unwilling to double back over our road, the only course left us to get back to the Union Pacific was to travel cross country. Our host, the sheepherder, volunteering to accompany us part of the way, we left camp at six. Soon we learned that he was no better informed than we were, and bade him adieu. We travelled over unbeaten paths and sheep trails in a rather aimless fashion until it occurred to us that if we hoped to reach our goal that day we must decide upon some more definite course. We finally decided to split up our party, each man taking a different direction, in the hope of finding some settlement which might assist us in locating ourselves, thus shaping our course. Matters looked rather hopeless, when suddenly one of our party shouted that he saw a team travelling along a road, which much to our surprise, was but a short distance off;

"SCOUTING". FINDING ROADS WITH THE ASSISTANCE OF A
SHEEPHERDER AND HIS HORSE

with an impassable gully between us however. We lost no time in hailing the driver,
who told us that we were but eighteen miles
from Hanna, on the Union Pacific, and that
if we followed the road he was on we would
have no further difficulties. Fortunately,
another of our party spied a structure of some
kind a mile or more off, which on investiga-
tion proved to be a deserted wooden corral.
Appropriating what lumber we needed, we
packed it to the gully, built a bridge, and
safely ran our car across and on to the road.
Consulting our clock and odometer we found
that we had consumed four hours covering
but six miles. Elated with our success in
finding a road and with a few miles of easy
running, we soon forgot our troubles, when
we were rudely awakened by more serious
trouble. We ran on to a road which at some
time must have been used for hauling ore,
with the result that the ruts cut into it resem-
bled gullies, impossible for our machine to
travel in. With one wheel on the hog back
of the road, the other on the high bank paralleling the road, we tried it for a way. This

failing, we left the road and travelled through the sagebrush, which we felt would, at the worst, not injure the fly wheel of the machine, if it did rip off its drip pan. There being no way out of our dilemma, we bowed to the inevitable, and travelled cautiously out of the sagebrush and into a flooded district. At half-past eleven that forenoon we finally reached Hanna, and were back to the line of the Union Pacific which, as previously stated, we were to follow. At Medicine Bow, twelve miles further on, we were told that the Medicine Bow River at Ware Ranch had overflowed its banks, and that it would not be advisable to attempt to ford it. This, however, did not deter us; for thinking the report an exaggerated one, we continued on our way. Arriving opposite Ware Ranch we hailed a man on horseback who happened to be nearby, and at the suggestion of one of our party requested him to ford the river with his horse so that we might get some idea of its depth, and help us to a conclusion. It was finally agreed that Mr. Diggles and I were to arrange for horses to accompany the machine. We

WARE RANCH, MEDICINE BOW

started off on our mission, leaving the others to busy themselves winding all the available rope we had aboard around the rim of the rear wheels, in order to give them traction. With some difficulty (not without getting our feet wet), Mr. Diggles and I reached the opposite bank and made our wants known, but before the horses were in readiness we saw our machine ploughing through the water to terra firma. After settling with the rancher and explaining to him that our party had brought the machine thus far under its own power, and that as a matter of pride we were anxious to so continue, we were off; but not for any great distance, for we soon found the road closed by barbed wire fences.

Retracing the Pioneers

Seeing some automobile tracks on the inside of the fence, we cut the wires, let our machine through, and in order to show our good breeding, perhaps also fearing the law, we replaced them as we found them, and regained our road. Soon after, and but a few miles out of Rock River, we met a party of autoists also bound East. We travelled in company as far as the Laramie River, where they stopped to take water. Leaving them we ran on another short stretch, when much to our disgust, we saw a lane ahead that in the words of the motorists, "did not look good to us". The sight of one of the New York-Seattle cars stuck in the mud made our hope of getting over this apparently bottomless road most dubious. Mr. Diggles and I, possibly because we were better shod than the others of our party, set out to take soundings, leaving the others to wind the rope around the rear wheels preparatory to venturing over the road. Satisfied that if our machine could get over this horrible stretch we could make Laramie for the night, we motioned our driver to come on. The feat safely accomplished, we stopped the machine and awaited the coming of the one we left behind us at the river. It was a comical sight to see it coming through the lane with its driver attempting to follow our irregular track. This done and feeling our services no longer needed, we again moved on, reaching Laramie at eight thirty-five that night, with our odometer at 121.7 miles.

$\mathcal{T}$IRED as a result of the previous, for us, most strenuous day's work, we did not leave Laramie for Cheyenne, a distance of 58.5 miles, till noon, a short but interesting run.

Out of Tie Siding, a short distance from Laramie, our attention was attracted by a sign put up by an enterprising rancher, reading: "Notice.— All automobiles going this road to Cheyenne must pay 50c. A. Borseman".

58

AMES BROS. MONUMENT

Retracing the Pioneers

We soon learned that the county road for some distance was impassable, and that the rancher, with an eye to business, insured safe travelling through his domain and on to the main highway, at a cost of fifty cents. It must not be supposed that he spent time or money improving the road through his ranch. In lieu of that he had a team of horses ready to haul machines out of trouble when required. Regaining the main highway, we climbed up to Sherman, at one time the highest point on the Union Pacific, but deserted since its reconstruction. At, or near Sherman, we saw a monument in the form of a pyramid erected to the memory of the Ames Bros., contractors and builders of the road. The monument stood close to a huge pile of rocks, itself much resembling a pyramid. We delayed long enough to take a few photographs, and then continued on to Granite Canyon and down the grade to Cheyenne.

61

Retracing the Pioneers

RUNNING over miserable roads and through a sparsely settled country had gotten on our nerves, and with joy we hailed the promise of better roads and a more thickly settled country through Nebraska, but forty-three miles further east. The country no doubt will, ere long, be a rich farming one; as yet it is merely land fenced in under homestead, but recently wrested from the big cattle owners. Each section boasted but a shack. Our introduction to Nebraska roads was disappointing, for at Bushnell, but a few miles from the Wyoming-Nebraska line, fearing to ford a creek, we ran over a bridge which was much the worse for the ravages of the water; the result being that one of its loose planks wrenched the fender and running board of our machine, recording the first accident of the journey. We soon saw that good roads were not to be our lot. Meeting a motor-party from Denver, after a pow-wow we concluded to make a detour to Kimball, in place of following the route along the railroad through a flooded district. From there we ran on to Sidney, our destination, having registered 111.6 miles for the day.

Retracing the Pioneers

OUT of Sidney we ran to Chappell, where we left the line of the Union Pacific for a better and more direct route to Big Springs. Owing to late rains we were compelled to make a number of detours which meant nothing more than the crossing and recrossing of the South Platte River, but this gave us a better opportunity to see the rich farming country of the South Platte. From Sutherland we ran for some distance between the North and South Platte Rivers to their confluence, a short way beyond the town of North Platte. Following the south side of the Platte River for forty-eight miles we crossed it, and ran into Gothenburg, having made 177 miles for the day; a good indication that the roads were not bad.

CROSSING THE PLATTE RIVER

Retracing the Pioneers

FRISCO-BOSTON SIGN

E had not travelled more than about thirty miles out of Gothenburg when we were treated to a heavy downpour of rain, with the result that what we had so often been told was soon to be demonstrated, namely: "The roads are fine when it does not rain". It did not require much rain to make the roads too slippery for safe travelling. We put chains on the rear wheels of our machine and worried along for about two miles into Lexington, where we put up awaiting the passing of the storm. The storm over, we purchased a second set of chains, which we placed on the front wheels as an extra precaution against skidding, and ventured out. When within four miles of Kearny we saw the well known " Frisco-Boston" sign, which marks the half way between those cities, 1733 miles. We, however, had travelled 2301.5 miles to reach this point. From here on we had good roads, making Grand Island for the night, our mileage for the day being 117.6 miles.

Retracing the Pioneers

LEAVING Grand Island we continued on our way through the very rich farming country of the Platte. The day was entirely without incidents. Cautious running, however, was necessary, owing to the condition of the roads due to the occasional showers we encountered. With our odometer at 150.5 miles, we ran into Omaha.

Retracing the Pioneers

OWING to the intense heat and thunder storms which did not promise passable roads, we delayed at Omaha. On the morning of the twenty-eighth day we read reports stating that the lower end of Council Bluffs across the Missouri River was under water. Thinking the reports exaggerated, we decided to start out and see for ourselves. Before leaving we met a party of women motorists who told us that their car was tied up in Vail, Iowa, and that they feared we would not be able to travel over the roads. Our minds made up, we started out at eleven that forenoon. The reports of the flooded district of Council Bluffs were soon verified, but the water having receded, we found no difficulty in making that city. We were not much further along when we found it necessary to put chains on the wheels of our car, and with our odometer at eleven miles we were stuck in Iowa's "Gumbo" (a wet, thick and heavy soil). Extricating our machine, we again got under way. Following along section lines to the west and north of the Boyer River, in order to avoid the flooded roads, we ran along slowly, feeling our way, when at dusk there appeared ahead of us a stretch of two hundred feet of road entirely under water and not at all promising. The tracks of a wagon that had but recently gone through the puddle, gave us courage, and without much hesitation, we ran in, and luckily, out of it. Plugging, as we had been, for an entire afternoon, we did not feel hilarious; but the spectators our machine attracted, as it travelled through the water, and their astonishment at not seeing us stuck, was most amusing. Though our objective point for the night was Dennison, with its good hotel, eight-fifteen saw us in Arion with anything but a good hotel, and with but 72.3 miles as the result of nine hours running. Here we were assured that owing to the country being under water and bridges out, we could proceed no further.

Retracing the Pioneers

AFTER an all but restful night we were up and about bright and early in search of road information. The night before, our proceeding further under our own power, as stated, looked hopeless. Search soon revealed an individual who claimed that on the previous day he had travelled over the stretch of road that was causing us so much thought. Following his instructions we put on our four chains and at eight that morning pulled out of Arion, and much to our chagrin found that we were but forty minutes in reaching Dennison, which the night previous we had been told was inaccessible from the west. At Vail, ten miles further on, we were again in a quandary as to the advisability of proceeding, knowing that a machine had been stalled in a marshy lane which we were to travel over. On the advice of a storekeeper we put our "mud fighters" on the wheels and "kept close to the fence". Our power pulled us through, and good luck saved the springs of the machine. From here we travelled under more or less difficulties, until we reached Ogden (Iowa), where a severe thunder storm assisted us in a conclusion to tie up, awaiting its passing. Under the impression if we were to fear any part of the road ahead of us, it would be near Boone, we 'phoned the garage proprietor at that place, asking him if he would advise us to come on. With an affirmative answer from him we started. Still, in spite of road conditions, we enjoyed the very rich farming country, and were agreeably surprised and pleased to find ourselves in a "dandy" forest, but a short way out on our way to Boone, which place we reached with our odometer at 95.6 miles.

"GUMBO" ROAD OUT OF VAIL, IOWA

Retracing the Pioneers

IOWA PASTORAL

E left Boone with the pleasing information that but a short run would see us on good roads. Fifteen miles out we ran into Ames, where we visited the State College and its beautiful grounds. Travelling on we noticed the difference in soil, and though not experts, we concluded that Eastern Iowa could not boast of as rich and productive a soil as the western half of the State, if it could boast of better roads.

At Tama, about sixty-five miles out of Ames, we ran on the promised good roads,

74

and the temptation being great we speeded on to Cedar Rapids; our odometer reading 136 miles for the day.

Retracing the Pioneers

LEAVING Cedar Rapids at seven twenty-five the next morning we took advantage of good roads, and at noon day had covered ninety-one miles, which saw us in Clinton.

After luncheon we crossed the Mississippi River and into Fulton, Ill. Continuing, we, at six twenty that evening, were in De Kalb.

With Chicago but sixty-three miles away, and being anxious to get there, we took on gas and soon were off again. Travelling after dark over strange roads made our progress slow; but at nine-thirty that night we reached Maywood. From there we travelled over the boulevards of Chicago to our hotel on Michigan Avenue, which place we made by ten-twenty that night, with two hundred and forty miles as the day's run.

APPROACH TO MISSISSIPPI RIVER BRIDGE

Retracing the Pioneers

ANXIOUS to reach our goal, New York City, we delayed but two days in Chicago. The morning of the thirty-fourth day saw us running out Michigan Avenue through Washington Park and by the Boulevard to Jackson Park, the site of the World's Columbian Exposition of 1893. A short visit to its few remaining interesting places, and away we were.

Leaving Jackson Park we were not long in making Hammond, where we entered Indiana.

Running over a rolling, wooded country, at two that afternoon we made the carriage and wagon manufacturing city, South Bend, for luncheon. Owing to heavy rains we, a short distance further, put into Goshen, with our odometer at 136 miles.

Retracing the Pioneers

AT an early hour the next morning we left Goshen, continuing through a wooded and farming country to the Indiana-Ohio State Line, a little beyond Butler, and to Toledo, a busy railroad center on the Maumee River.

After a half hour at Toledo we proceeded, and with our odometer at 176.4 miles ran into Fremont.

Retracing the Pioneers

SINCE leaving Chicago we had travelled by aid of the Rand-McNally "Photo Auto Guide". At Fremont we were told that the "Automobile Blue Book" offered a choice of routes. The weather being in our favor, we chose the Lake Shore route. Seven and a half miles out of Fremont, at Clyde, we headed north, and at Hudson, twenty-five and a half miles further, ran on to the "Lake Road". Following the Lake front over good roads, and through a vineyard country for nigh forty-eight miles, brought us into Cleveland.

Leaving Cleveland, we continued on the "Lake Shore Road" out Euclid Avenue. Ninety-eight miles of excellent running and with 179.3 miles for the day's run, we were in Erie, Pennsylvania.

Retracing the Pioneers

THE next morning at about eight we left Erie, and after a run of but eighteen and a half miles, through a vineyard country, we reached the Pennsylvania-New York State Line. Following along the south shore of Lake Erie we at noon day ran into Buffalo, our odometer registering 91.3 miles.

A PENNSYLVANIA ROAD

Retracing the Pioneers

HAVING covered over two thousand miles since our car received its last careful overhauling, and with enough of interest in and about Buffalo to hold us for a couple of days, we did not leave that city until the morning of the fortieth day.

We were not further than about eight miles from our hotel when, running at a speed of twenty-two miles, we were stopped by a constable, who, acting as arresting officer, judge and jury, taxed us ten dollars for exceeding the State speed limit.

Seventy-four miles of good running, saw us in Rochester on the Genesee River. Desirous of seeing the lakes of northern New York State, we travelled southeast from Rochester to Canandaigua, and to the lake of the same name. Sixteen miles further, we ran into Geneva, on Seneca Lake, and but eleven miles more, just out of Seneca Falls, we were in sight of Cayuga Lake. After travelling over the Montezuma swamp we soon were in Auburn, where, owing to the lateness of the hour, we left the lake district and travelled northeast, and with 172.9 miles as our odometer reading, ran into Syracuse.

Retracing the Pioneers

STONE TOLL ROAD BETWEEN SYRACUSE AND FAYETTEVILLE, N. Y.

ITH the exception of the previous afternoon's run from Canandaigua to Auburn, New York State did not afford us anything other than good roads. The trees we saw appeared to us to be affected by a blight. We feared that possibly our long journey across the continent had begun to make us indifferent to our surroundings, when but a short way out of Utica and but fifty miles from Syracuse, which city we left that morning at nine, we ran into the Valley of the Mohawk, whose beauties soon hauled us out of our reveries. At Little Falls, twenty-two miles further east, the view of the Mohawk, the Erie Canal and the railways wending their way side by side through a narrow gorge cut through a spur of the Adirondacks by the River, we were more than awakened to the beauties of the often referred to " Valley of the Mohawk ". Continuing along the Mohawk and the canal for a distance of nearly fifty-seven miles we reached Schenectady. A run of fourteen and a half miles without strict observance of the State's speed law soon saw us in Albany, on the Hudson, with 142.4 miles for our day's run.

Retracing the Pioneers

MONUMENT ON NEW YORK STATE ROAD

EAVING Albany we crossed the Hudson to Rensselaer and on to the State Road, which runs along the east side of the River. This we soon learned was a river road in name only. To our dismay it afforded us but infrequent views of the Hudson. Disappointed, we tried the lower roads which skirt the river. These not being continuous, we returned to the State Road and followed it to Poughkeepsie, a distance of seventy-four miles from Albany. From here we expected we would no longer have to content ourselves with occasional glimpses of the river, but not until we reached Peekskill, thirty-four miles further south, did we get unobstructed views of the Hudson. Travelling through a succession of villages we were soon in sight of the Palisades, and entered the City of New York at Two Hundred and Thirtieth Street, thence to the Riverside Drive, which we followed to its end, on to the busy thoroughfares, and with 148.9 miles for the day we pulled up at our hotel in Times Square. Our run across the American Continent was accomplished. With a registered mileage of 4088.5 miles the machine was delivered at the wharf ready for the crate which was to house it on its voyage across the Atlantic, and we were looking forward to our European trip which was to follow.

TIMES SQUARE, NEW YORK CITY

Transcontinental Itinerary

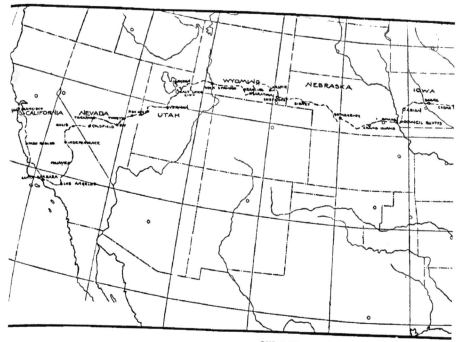

OUR ROUTE FROM SAN FRANCISCO TO NEW YO

Transcontinental Itinerary

Roads good; several grades

TIME		MILES
8.00 A. M.	San Francisco, Cal. (Mission Dolores) *via* Mission Road	
9.00	San Mateo	18.8
0.21	San Jose	49.
1.28	Gilroy	77.2
	San Juan *via* San Juan Grade . .	
1.05 P. M.	Salinas	105.5
3.05	Soledad	130.
4.50	Jolon	167.
	via Indian Valley	
	San Miguel	
7.45	Paso Robles	221.5

221.5

June 2, 1909.

'ood and bad roads. Many gullies along the coast. Some grades.

8.13 A. M.	Paso Robles	
9.58	San Luis Obispo	30.2
1.02 .	Arroyo Grande *via* Pismo	46.2
1.55	Nipomo	54.5
2.25 P. M.	Santa Maria	61.5
4.18	Los Olivos	95.6
8.15	Santa Barbara *via* Gaviota . . .	147.8

369.3

June 3, 1909.

Two grades. Roads good.

8.35 A. M.	Santa Barbara	
0.42	Ventura	33.8
2.10 P. M.	Los Angeles, cor. 4th and Spring Streets	107.9

477.2

Retracing the Pioneers

June 5, 1909.

Fair roads.

TIME		MILES	
7.00 A. M.	Los Angeles		
7.55	Fernando	21.9	
10.55	Palmdale *via* Soledad Canyon . . .	68.9	
12.10 P. M.	Del Sur	84.	
	Willow Springs	100.5	
3.15	Mojave	114.6	
			51.8

June 6, 1909.

Poor roads. Many stretches of sand.

5.20 A. M.	Mojave		
6.20	Cinco	17.3	
7.20	Ricardo	26.3	
	Grape Vine	53.7	
10.30	Little Lake	67.9	
11.30	Haiwee	84.7	
2.30 P. M.	Olancha	93.6	
4.20	Lone Pine	116.9	
5.50	Independence	132.5	
			724.3

June 7, 1909.

Fair roads. Several grades. Toll at Toll House, White Mountains.

6.55 A. M.	Independence		
8.50	Big Pine	27.2	
10.10	White Mountains (Toll House) . .	35.5	
11.20	Gilbert Ranch	53.7	
12.25 P. M.	Oasis, Cal.	65.3	
2.30	California-Nevada line	67.5	
4.00	Silver Peak, Nevada	91.2	
6.15	Goldfield	128.2	
			852.5

June 8, 1909.

Fair roads.

10.30 A. M.	Goldfield		
12.00 noon	Tonopah	25.6	
			878.1

Transcontinental Itinerary

JUNE 9, 1909.

Sand for short stretches; good and bad roads.

TIME			MILES
;.05 A. M.	Tonopah		
).40	Stone Cabin	36.8	
3.35	Warm Springs	52.6	
).12	Twin Springs	62.6	
2.56 P. M.	Blue Eagle	114.5	
2.55	Curry Creek	127.1	
5.40	Barnes	153.6	
7.15	Ely	181.	
7.25	East Ely	182.6	
		——	1060.7

JUNE 10, 1909.

Good roads.

2.30 P. M.	East Ely		
3.20	McGill	11.4	
5.13	Schellbourne	40.3	
8.15	Tippett	67.7	
		——	1128.4

JUNE 11, 1909.

Alkali flats, ditches and generally poor roads.

7.50 A. M.	Tippett, Nevada		
9.15	Nevada-Utah line	10.2	
0.07	Deep Creek, Utah	23.5	
0.15	Ibapah	25.2	
2.15 P. M.	Callao (Willow Springs)	49.4	
3.30	Fish Springs (Thomas)	70.0	
		——	1199.3

JUNE 12, 1909.

Fair desert roads.

5.15 A. M.	Fish Springs (Thomas)		
0.05	Simpson	41.1	
4.00 P. M.	Lookout	57.1	
6.45	Vernon	65.6	
		——	1264.0

VERNON, JUNE 13, 1909.

Retracing the Pioneers

Fair Roads.

TIME		MILES
2.50 P. M.	Vernon	
3.30	Ajax	11.6
4.15	Stockton	25.5
4.40	Tooele	31.9
5.25	Lakepoint	46.2
5.35	Smelter	48.4
5.40	Garfield	50.2
6.30	Salt Lake City	66.2
		——— 1331.1

SALT LAKE CITY, JUNE 15, 1909.
JUNE 16, 1909.
Roads fair and good.

TIME		MILES
10.10 A. M.	Salt Lake City	
10.45	Bountiful	9.6
11.07	Farmington	15.9
11.25	Kaysville	20.7
11.35	Layton	23.
11.50	Clearfield	27.8
12.10 P. M.	Riverdale	33.9
12.25	Ogden	36.7
	Riverdale	40.4
3.38	Peterson	56.9
4.05	Morgan	64.3
5.	Devil's Slide	72.4
5.45	Henefer	79.2
6.	Echo	83.
7.15	Castle Rock	99.4
7.50	Wahsatch, Utah	107.7
8.10	Utah-Wyo. Line	113.2
8.35	Evanston, Wyo.	117.7
		——— 1448.8

JUNE 17, 1909.
Roads bad and very bad; many gullies (washes).

TIME		MILES
8.40 A. M.	Evanston	
10.55	So. Cumberland	32.3
	No. Cumberland	34.8
11.45	Glencoe	40.8
1.10 P. M.	Opal	58.5
3.50	Granger	83.6
	Marston Wash	93.5
6.55	Green River	116.4
8.	Rock Springs	131.3
		——— 1580.1

Transcontinental Itinerary

June 18, 1909.

Stretches of sand; number of gullies; bad roads.

TIME			MILES
7.45 A. M.	Rock Springs	
9.20	Point of Rocks	25.2
1. P. M.	Bitter Creek	47.8
2.45	Table Rock	57.6
3.15	Tipton	64.4
3.50	Red Desert	71.6
4.25	Wamsutter	80.4
7.05	Daly Ranch	100.5
8.05	Rawlins	123.
			—— 1703.1

June 19, 1909.

Fair and good roads; very bad roads; detour of 40 miles owing to flood (Rawlins to Hanna).

8.35 A. M.	Rawlins	
12.05 P. M.	Saratoga	39.2
2.25	Schoojan's Ranch	53.3
5.	Elk Mtns. (open country)	57.4
			—— 1760.5

June 20, 1909.

Roads very bad.

6.15 A. M.	Elk Mtns. (open country)	
11.35	Hanna	25.
1.05 P. M.	Carbon	36.8
1.50 .	Medicine Bow	47.2
3.10	Ware Ranch	50.3
5.10	Rock River	66.7
8.35	Laramie	121.7
			—— 1882.2

June 21, 1909.

Roads generally not bad; bad in spots.

12.45 P. M.	Laramie	
1.35	Tie Siding	18.3
2.15	Sherman	25.8
	Buford	31.5
3.15	Granite Canyon	39.7
4.30	Cheyenne	58.5
			—— 1940.7

99

Retracing the Pioneers

June 22, 1909.

Roads good when it does not rain.

TIME			MILES
9.25 A. M.	Cheyenne		
11.33	Egbert	32.3	
12.15 P. M.	Pine Bluff, Wyo.	42.2	
1.20	Smeed, Neb.	48.	
1.50	Bushnell	52.6	
2.15	Kimball	75.1	
4.25	Potter	93.1	
5.25	Sidney	111.6	
		———	2052.3

June 23, 1909.

Roads good when it does not rain.

TIME		MILES	
7.15 A. M.	Sidney		
8.20	Lodge Pole	18.	
8.55	Chappell	37.5	
10.25	Big Springs	59.2	
11.25	Brule	72.9	
11.55	Ogallala	83.3	
2. P. M.	Paxton	103.7	
2.35	Sutherland	115.8	
4.15	No. Platte	138.9	
5.25	Bignell	152.5	
7.10	Gothenburg	177.	
		———	2229.3

June 24, 1909.

Roads good when it does not rain.

TIME		MILES	
7.15 A. M.	Gothenburg		
7.55	Cozad	13.9	
9.15	Lexington	31.9	
1.50 P. M.	Elm Creek	56.1	
2.30	Frisco-Boston Sign	68.	
2.50	Kearny	72.2	
3.30	Shelton	91.2	
3.55	Wood River	99.	
4.40	Grand Island	117.6	
		———	2346.9

Transcontinental Itinerary

JUNE 25, 1909.

Roads good when it does not rain.

TIME			MILES
7.45 A. M.	Grand Island	. . . .	
8.30	Chapman .	. . . .	12.9
9.20	Central City	. . . .	23.2
0.00	Clarks	. . . .	34.1
0.45	Silver Creek	. . . .	45.2
2.00 Noon	Columbus	. . . .	64.9
	Benton	. . . .	73.5
	Schuyler	. . . .	81.4
2.55 P. M.	Rogers	. . . .	89.5
4.15	Fremont	. . . .	112.2
	Waterloo	. . . .	130.5
5.45	Elkhorn	. . . .	133.6
6.35	Omaha	. . . .	150.5

————— 2497.4

OMAHA, NEB., June 26 and 27, 1909.

JUNE 28, 1909.

¯oll *Missouri River bridge; "Gumbo" roads are almost impassable when it rains.*

1.15 A. M.	Omaha, Nebraska	. . . . . .	
1.35	Council Bluffs, Iowa	. . . .	5.1
1.45 P. M.	Honey Creek .	. . . . . .	18.3
2.40	Missouri Valley	. . . . . .	27.3
3.55	Logan	. . . .	36.6
5.15	Woodbine	. . . . . .	47.3
8.15	Arion .	. . . .	72.3

————— 2569.7

JUNE 29, 1909.

Roads good if it does not rain. "Gumbo Soil."

8.05 A. M.	Arion .	. . . . . .	
8.50	Dennison .	. . . . . .	8.9
0.20	Vail	. . . .	18.8
1.15	West Side	. . . . . .	24.8
2.10 P. M.	Carroll	. . . . . .	37.1
1.20	Glidden	. . . . . .	44.8
2.	Scranton	. . . . . .	56.2
2.40	Jefferson	. . . . . .	66.5
3.	Grand Junction	. . . . . .	74.3
3.50	Ogden	. . . . . .	85.6
6.15	Boone .	. . . . . .	95.6

————— 2665.3

Retracing the Pioneers

Roads good if it does not rain. "Gumbo soil." From Tama roads good.

TIME		MILES	
8.05 A. M.	Boone		
9.30	Ames	15.3	
10.10	Nevada	24.8	
11.25	State Center	39.8	
12.15 P. M.	Marshalltown	54.7	
	Le Grand	64.9	
	Montour	69.	
2.45	Tama	80.4	
	Gladstone	85.	
	Chelsea	91.8	
4.	Belle Plaine	100.	
5.45	Cedar Rapids	136.	
			2801.3

Toll: Mississippi River—Lyon-Fulton bridge; roads good.

TIME		MILES	
7.25 A. M.	Cedar Rapids		
7.50	Marion	5.8	
8.25	Mt. Vernon	18.9	
9.	Mechanicsville	30.2	
9.35	Clarence	41.2	
10.30	Lowden	49.8	
10.55	Wheatland	55.9	
11.20	Grand Mound	66.1	
12.30 P. M.	Clinton, Iowa	91.3	
2.	Fulton, Ill.	94.6	
3.	Morrison	106.6	
3.45	Sterling	121.2	
4.20	Dixon	134.5	
5.10	Ashton	149.	
5.40	Rochelle	160.	
6.20	De Kalb	177.5	
7.45	Geneva	203.	
	West Chicago	208.7	
9.30	Maywood	227.8	
10.20	Chicago (Michigan and Jackson Blvds)	240.	
			3041.3

Transcontinental Itinerary

oads good; traveled via Michigan City; via La Porte the shorter run.

TIME			MILES
8.30 A. M.	Chicago, Ill.	
9.05	Hammond, Ind.	24.2
9.50	Hobart	42.4
1.30	Valparaiso	55.4
	Westville	
	Michigan City	
2. P. M.	South Bend	112.1
4.35	Goshen	136.

——— 3177.3

JULY 5, 1909.
Roads good.

7.10 A. M.	Goshen	
8.	Ligonier	17.7
	Wawaka	24.
8.50	Kendallville	36.
	Waterloo	50.
	Butler, Ind.	58.
	Edgerton, Ohio	64.8
1.05	Bryan	76.4
	Archbold	91.3
	Wauseon	101.4
3.05 P. M.	Toledo	143.4
	Woodville	161.8
5.25	Fremont	176.4

——— 3353.7

JULY 6, 1909.
Toll at Conneaut river bridge; roads good.

7. A. M.	Fremont	
7.15	Clyde	7.5
7.40	Castalia	18.1
8.30	Huron	33.1
9.10	Vermillion	44.1
9.40	Lorain	54.6
9.55	Rocky River	73.1
1.25	Cleveland	81.1
1.45 P.M.	Willoughby	99.4
2.20	Painesville	109.8
3.05	Geneva	126.7
3.30	Ashtabula	135.7
4.10	Conneaut, Ohio	149.6
4.20	W. Springfield, Pa.	153.6
4.50	Girard	163.
5.	Fairview	166.8
5.40	Erie	179.3

——— 3533.0

Retracing the Pioneers

JULY 7, 1909.
Roads good.

TIME			MILES
7.50 A. M.	Erie, Pa.		
8.35	Northeast	15.	
8.45	State Line, N. Y.	18.6	
9.15	Westfield	30.3	
9.50	Fredonia	45.1	
10.25	Silver Creek	56.6	
12. Noon	Buffalo	91.3	
			3624.3

BUFFALO, N. Y., JULY 8 AND 9, 1909.

JULY 10, 1909.
Roads good.

TIME			MILES
7.40 A. M.	Buffalo		
9.35	Batavia	38.3	
	Bergen	54.2	
	Churchville	57.6	
11.30	Rochester	74.	
	Mendon	91.	
	Victor	96.3	
2.45 P. M.	Canandaigua	106.3	
3.30	Geneva	122.5	
	Waterloo	129.2	
4.15	Seneca Falls	132.7	
5.05	Auburn	147.4	
6.30	Syracuse	172.9	
			3797.2

JULY 11, 1909.
Roads good.

Two toll stations between Syracuse and Fayetteville (Stone road); toll crossing Mohawk river at Schenectady.

TIME			MILES
0. A. M.	Syracuse		
	Fayetteville	7.2	
12. Noon	Utica	48.8	
12.40 P. M.	Herkimer	63.9	
2.	Little Falls	71.	
	St. Johnsville	81.7	
3.40	Fonda	101.6	
4.20	Amsterdam	112.1	
5.15	Schenectady	127.8	
5.50	Albany	142.4	
			3939.6

104

Transcontinental Itinerary

Toll crossing Hudson river; roads good, mostly macadam. The "Post Road" along the Hudson does not afford any view of the Hudson river until Poughkeepsie is reached.

TIME		MILES
7.50 A. M.	Albany	
7.57	Rensselaer	1.4
9.10	Kinderhook	20.8
10.05	Hudson	33.1
11.20	Rhinebeck	57.8
1.10 P. M.	Poughkeepsie	73.9
3.10	Peekskill	107.6
5.15	Yonkers	134.1
6.15	New York City (Times Square) . .	148.9
		——— 4088.5

Record of mileage somewhat inaccurate owing to detours often necessary.

Time record does not show delays.

Total mileage: 4088.5.

Running time: 315 hours 37 minutes.

Gas consumed: 449 gallons.

Oil consumed: 48¼ gallons.

H34   ⟨5

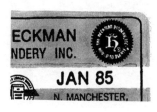